SUNSET GRILL

Anne Rouse was born in Washington, DC, in 1954, and raised in rural Virginia. After graduating from high school she worked at a variety of jobs, including house painting and installing equipment in telephone exchanges. The latter job required her to travel between small towns in Virginia and North Carolina.

In 1974 she came to England to study history at Bedford College, University of London, from which she took an honours degree in 1978. After a further year of doctoral research she enrolled as a student nurse in North London, obtaining her SRN and RMN qualifications. She became active in trade unionism, as a NUPE steward, and in local health politics. Since 1986 she has worked for the mental health charity MIND in Islington, where she lives.

Her poems have appeared in Britain and America in papers and magazines such as the *Atlantic Monthly, London Review of Books, New Statesman* and *The Observer*, and she has also published articles in *The Independent* and the *Washington Post*. A selection of her poems appeared in Carol Rumens' anthology *New Women Poets* (Bloodaxe Books, 1990). Her first collection, *Sunset Grill* (Bloodaxe Books, 1993), is a Poetry Book Society Recommendation.

SUNSET GRILL

Anne Rouse

BLOODAXE BOOKS

ISBN: 1 85224 219 1

First published 1993 by
Bloodaxe Books Ltd,
P.O. Box 1SN,
Newcastle upon Tyne NE99 1SN.

Bloodaxe Books Ltd acknowledges
the financial assistance of Northern Arts.

Cover printing by J. Thomson Colour Printers Ltd, Glasgow.

Printed in Great Britain by
Cromwell Press Ltd, Melksham, Wiltshire.

To Irene & Bill Rouse
and
Bill & Betty Sillett

Acknowledgements

Acknowledgements are due to the editors of the following publications in which some of these poems first appeared: *Atlantic Monthly, Encounter, The Honest Ulsterman, Kent Companion, London Magazine, London Review of Books, New Statesman, The Observer, Poetry Book Society Anthology 3* (PBS/Hutchinson, 1992), *Quartz, Toronto Life* and *Verse*. Nine of these poems were published in Carol Rumens' anthology *New Women Poets* (Bloodaxe Books, 1990).

Contents

A North London Planetary System

MERCURY *at Nags Head*

Sprawled in a flying squad transit van,
He's a wordy git, more mouth than sense.
Sunshine, it will all go down as evidence.

The eyelids flick. Dead air, tough luck.
Our verbals judder through the grille.
It's hot back there: reinforced steel

But he's miles off, floored from the heat
And spent lead, with a look that may be
Used against him. The bastard is happy.

VENUS *on Holloway Road*

The low wonder of the firmament
Slips a vial of perfume
Down her blonde provincial mac,

To fool the flatfoot by the doors,
That pleasure better circulates
And breathes:

The black kiss-curls like hooks,
The walk a local incident
While a loitering sun

Touches her on the thoroughfare.
Praise Venus.
This is her free gift.

EARTH *(Seven Sisters Road)*

They buy less now to season, more from mood.
We throw away as much as sell.
Whatever's ripe we put on special.

I get my son to shout,
A pound a pound. Safeways never shut.
Freshness goes in artificial light.

I've been robbed, seen fights, stood
Through freezing rain. You hear
Some things. I've heard it all round here.

MARS *(Arsenal)*

His is the red inversion
Of your flesh, Venus;
BASTARDS, is the heart's tattoo,

And the blood's thunder
Who feels his young love
Liquefy in terror

Having fulfilled, with distinction,
Some stale official order's
Every clause.

JUPITER *(Liverpool Road)*

'Madame J is throwing a party,'
Blares a northern voice. 'Next door's
Miserable bitch will get us busted for noise.
Christ, what a comedown from Macao as a bride,
Where the flash Harry ditched me and the local
Chief of Police showed his private collection
Of choice contraband gear to me with the
Twenty inch waist and the looks of a filmstar,
Clinically trained, a beautician and nanny:
He offered to buy me a Portuguese penthouse...
Tenner a bedroom, mixers supplied.'

Mercury trades his cannabis and flies;
Saturn passing, rubs a shaven jaw;
Young Mars needs cash but has a go
At Venus, standing just inside the door.

SATURN *at Hornsey Road*

Mr Saturn is wanted on the telephone.
There is a number for the other business
In the car or – if urgent – with the mistress,
Or he may be on his portable at the Ouzo café.

When there is a rush on; when there are orders
For the summer frocks, and aching eyes
And shoulders, the women may be comforted
On the rounds of the machines

By his casual icon, who – alert-breasted
Under a lush fountain streaming,
A Titaness from a magazine – surveys them
Fondly, as his light-tempered foreman.

NEPTUNE *in Finsbury Park*

He's been a hand
On every sea,
Navvied in ports.
The gulls winter
Down the estuary.
He stumps the inland course
Of hostels and DSS,
Missing the dawns
And the absence of people,
His uphill walk
Too stiff for pity;
His wants shrunk
To an infallible kit.

URANUS *(Archway)*

Forgive us the furthest radiant of sorrow,
Where the child was last seen and the
Occasional evil circulates, frozen;
The time she can never make up
From that mania or this despair:
The woman who loses her children
To care, or the murdering lover.
Look, how the actor moves but the act
Disseminates, a grey sift raining
On us; have mercy: the hands that
Are raised bear the scars on each arm.

PLUTO *(Highbury)*

I've seen him wandering
The roundabout, and frozen station.

If Hermes Whisperer repeats the world,
To what does he return?

12

A Singer

When she brought out her lyrics
And twanged her odd bow,
She left the voters averse
And the authorities shaken.

Suave agents in limousines,
A bellhop, the bar help,
A QC in his wig, mid-summation,
Saw themselves broken

By particular lives
Between rock and stone.
The city fell; the Fleet sank;
In Soho no punters were taken.

Men cried over the tannoys,
'This my one life,'
Feeling horror at beggers and news.
When her mantra was spoken,

Vaults cracked, alarms failed,
And the secretaries printing out
On their Amstrads, 'all journeys lead home',
Prayed for a hero to take on

The singer and cap the bold song
Like an oil-rig on fire,
In hopes that the extraordinary
Would leave them alone.

Hurt

A great hurt is waiting in the room.
– We could catch a movie if we're quick.
– This drink tastes nice,
What did you say you called it?

Anything other
Than square up to the lightless eyes
Of hurt, like a tall indescribable baby
Whose past is becoming the future, too;

Anything other than saying, gentle now,
I'll let you, hurt, I'll stay,
And waking up to the chilling sheets,
Flat and lost as after a failed operation,

And walking the avenues alone
With the dim-witted solace of morning.

Her Retirement

Just a little party, nothing swank,
I told the founder, but you know Mr B.
There are so many of you here to thank.

I leave you the later tube trains, dank
At the hand-rails from a human sea,
Dreaming down to Morden via Bank.

I've homed quietly to port while others sank,
By keeping at my stenography.
There are so many of you here to thank.

I scan the backs of houses, rank on rank:
The comfy lamps, the oblique misery
Streaming down to Morden via Bank.

Our gardens keep us from the abyss, I think.
With the cheque I'll buy a trellis, or a tree.
There are so many of you here to thank.

And unaccustomed as I am to drink,
I toast you all who follow me
– There are so many of you here to thank –
In dreaming down to Morden, via Bank.

Nightside

When a body's anger
Sharpens to sex;
When the brain's bestiary
Resolves to it,
And from the furthest
Lake – a caldera
Between mountains –
Thrusts upwards, dripping,
This,
Then who dreams
Of the one warm beside?

But if that one goes,
And the horizon
Torques and twists,
Widdershins,
So that the known world
Flips, what
Does a body do, but sink
In dreaming's furrow,
As if the past's
Warm reek returns
At sorrow?

M3

Mean as a length of flex, it snubs the B road,
Disliking breakdown and hiker, impedimenta;
Droning the highway code
At shuddering lorries, and the reps for shampoo,
Blurring southward to the postcard rack
And coffee on the lido.

As time stripped down to mere emergency,
It tarmacs older memories of sense,
Of littering picnic; of plum tree,
Rooks, and manure,
Nerves like a harp in the blown high grass.
Inland, it simply hands over.

Botany

Calmly you say, 'It is a begonia.'
Your sick husband tends the beanflowers,
The honeysuckle aspiring to the mesh fence,
Leaving you to entertain its passion.
It has drawn itself up like an apache dancer.
The sunflower cocks a head, and the émigré poppies
Blister with their malice.
One could live like this for years,
In the deaf lull before the riot.
But it turns vivid, with the failed light,
As blood. We watch through glass.
None of us knows how it will turn out.

Miss North Crawley

It was a whirlwind year
For Miss North Crawley
Of 1971:

Viv won the booty –
The cheque and the fortnight
In Lanzarote.

At every spring gala,
She presided in Jaeger
With Hermes umbrella.

Meanwhile her neighbour
And husband had struck on
A mutual favour.

Viv never shouted,
But down at the Saracen
Desperately flirted.

During her sway
In swim suit and spiked heels
Down the gangway

For the roaring punters,
She'd seen a face
Less foolish than others –

He was drinking that day.
He drove her home,
Singing 'Be My Baby'.

By July she'd decided
They'd run away south.
The Hillman was loaded.

He walked off ahead
When she started the row,
Through a stubbled field

Outside Crawley proper
Where year on year,
The drifts of her hair

And her small perfect teeth
Bleach in the air.

Nude Descending a Stair

Their pornographic tryst
Ran in pauses, and resumptions,
As the lit windows of a train
Will repeat a silhouette,
Looking out on brave cafés
And tin fly-posted shops.

Both were 'fully participant'.
A month or more would pass
Abjuring the telephone
For the long peace back-to-back:
Whoever turned around
Guessed at the other's mind.

They can stroll the earth
Where the horizon bends
Innocent as friends –
Among the blue-shadowed curves
And angles of the room,
What is missing, is the nude.

The Madam

We wanted to be tough, to rope the bleating rams
Into a dread spectacular!
The last raid on the house felt like a game.
I preferred prison meals and circuit walks
To waiting here at home – a lifer's sentence.

Our crowd was groping in an alley
Through carnivals of vaseline, of leather.
One old boy would cry and we grew tired.
(We had to love them so much less than money.)
But even so they needed it:

The reddened room and in the driver's seat
A girl, whose husband beat her for a joke.
The body's ludicrous. We tried for style,
Until they ran me down this cul-de-sac
In dressing-gown, a PC at each side,

And only were not secretive or vile, enough.

Cat Fancy

This Hampshire weekend the Farthingales,
Dreaming on the C-shape of the pool,
Overlook a cat come prowling
Along the tiny flickers of the waves.
It noses a reflection; dives –
The first shock of their marriage.

A wet cat stink jeers from the pine fence;
Pawprints, four of clubs, mar the paving stones.
But you can't lay traps, or unleash a dog
On a rolled and weeded lawn.

Missus fetches from the house the Fairy Liquid
And squeezes out declivities and mounds of foam,
Through which the cat bobs, blithely circling;

But Mister has just achieved promotion
After epics of guile and badinage,
Springing for an Audi and the swimming pool,

So that when the cat regains the rim –
Slyly hunched,
And sporting raffish facial tufts –
Mister, momentarily fleet,
Runs round and kicks it.

The tom squalls out of touch
Behind some begonias
From which it creeps balefully as Richard the Third,
To whoosh like gale-blown fluff up the garden trellis.

Peace enchants them, the peace of tumblers and lounge chairs.
No satyr's flute, nor even monotonous hedge-trimmings
Trouble the afternoon.
At the pearling of dusk they retire.

Rankness leaps at them;
Swallows the pink air-freshening wick in the loo;
Upends the pot-pourri,

And nightly a caterwaul begins
Sounding down the hours the nine cacophonous lives;
Frightening the moles and the sparrows.

Pools

He told a tolerant mike that things wouldn't change much.
Caught in the cameras' freeze, through the chat
And clink of the milling PR boys,
The wife stood working his hand like billyo.

Are you a winner? a magazine asked. He'd said no.
Behind the TV a generous sun touched a hill
As they'd hushed, listening for the child's cry.
Consoles and bedroom suites lined up to cheer.

They broke through the door, led by the wide-toothed compère.
The sky was uncannily white, the sky that a newt puzzles under,
Circling its grass-lined bowl.
With her arm in his, he mumbled it would be all right.

Baby Tony at Al's Cafe

The gangling child, outgrowing babyhood
Lolls on his pushchair, a seaside toff.
Fate's pinned him here as audience
To the waiter's act with knives,
And left a consoling bottle out of reach.
His pre-prandial remarks conclude
In a surging *Dies Irae*: the waiter,
A family man, retrieves it where it lies.
Babe slugs it back, fish-eyed through the smoke.
His mother pauses from volubility to dote,
Swooping aside before the sentence drops.
Our man has tasted everything once.
He gets another chip, tests it with his mouth,
Rolling it slowly round like a panatella.

England Nil

The advance to Hamburg broke with all the plans.
Doug spelled them out in Luton Friday night.
Someone had ballsed it up. A dozen vans
Waited in convoy, ringside. Blue and white
We stumbled through. The beer
When we found it in that piss-hole of jerries
Was all we needed. Who won the war,
Anyway? Who nuked Dresden? Two fairies
Skittered behind the bar, talking Kraut
Or maybe Arabic. We clocked the poison
Smiles and chanted till the SS threw us out.
Stuttgart was a tea-party to this. One
By one they've nicked us, berserk with fear.
You've been Englished but you won't forget it, never.

A Birthday

So glad that your especial sperm
Pin-pricked your unequalled egg,
Promptly welcomed by your Mum,
Flushed and certain of your Dad's
Devotion.

So glad also the parties met,
And that a trillion forebears lived
Long enough to do the deed,
And that the first amoeba stirred
Its jelly head.

So glad that H linked twice with O;
That earth was favoured by the sun;
And that the present Total blew
From budding light, or like a bomb.

So glad you're here.

Belt

I like a belt, but only buckled round me.
Undone it's hazardous as lechery or hanging,
A mad snake, dreaded in fathers.
The hard tooth bites.
It leaves a dance of weals.

But this one is harmless on a cupboard rack.
You call to me, face upturned, laughing
At what you'd forgotten.
I loop it in coils around my fist and throw.
You catch it neatly in the front garden

To stop trousers falling, or finish off a look.
You astonish the neighbour's boy
With the sudden fumbling:
Lifting your jacket like grey wings,
Girding your loins for work.

Christmas Break

We've floored it from London.
The bridge winches up; the moat bares
To green algae silk, kitchen relics,
The bones of suicides.

The snow, fine as bride's
Fine lace, stacks up its trousseau:
A terrain in bedsheets, smoothed from memory.
The town's dead as midnight.

Rushing the houses of the estate,
The wind skims the roof
Like a bruising hand.
From now, a dining-table

Accommodates six at Scrabble
And a week's career beneath
The fairy lights: a family circuit
Closing like a wreath.

A Day Out in Berkshire

The trundling air balloon turns and preens
Against blue clemency. The buds were metal
When we crouched here among the fag-ends,

A late day when you turned aside
At the station platform, with boy's eyes:
It was warmer then than now, warm

As when a woman wooed a snake
That whispered to her – *time* – and slid,
A tremor in the fields, a single track.

Then Adam had to die, to save the crops;
Eve ruled, a goddess but not immortal,
And love sleeps in its attenuated state

Of splendour after the rosé, two good bottles;
You anchored in my blood, dumb dream-boat,
Not telling why I have to dream instead.

Burst

The sort of place that waits to become someone's past,
Is Lugworth Council's Mental Health Drop-in Centre.
She moves through the invisible hunched backs and stigmata
With the sanctity of the fit.
He attends irregularly, in a suit;
Carries her globular cameo back to his flat.

He's not that daft: she's a Tokyo Rose, hybrid, trained for this.
You could follow her voice for months without connection.
One bland day he sees her shopping with the mythical husband.
Both hello generously, not realising the transgression,
And the damned thing bursts over his part of the building,
A godawful mess but too thin even to drown in.

Sacrificial Wolf

The careful suburban dead turn their backs
On this squat of sodden grass,
Hedged by the Finchley traffic:
The vicar poised like a prowhead
Over the shameless pit, answered
By a hectoring gull. It brings back
The afternoons in the dry houses,
The hostels and clinic waiting-rooms,
When you with the cor anglais of a shout
Parted the smokers' fug,
Flattering social workers with quotes
From Wilde or Krishnamurti –
Such was the splendour and disgrace
That only a few of us have come to light
Our makeshift Roman candles, bitten shy:
An elegy, my friend, dear wolf,
Being just your sort of con.

Night Song

Our own death will be someone's
Milestone, whether we are teenaged,
Riding pillion on grown-up machines,
Or old, hoping 'they'll find a cure'.

Newscasters salt each dish with it,
The glandular fear of the secret hero,
The suicide, and the wife left to wonder
What he was thinking mid-air.

The middle-aged dears musing down
The slope of the garden to the canal
Embrace a sexy Catholicism.
A dosser drinks his last sense blurred.

It sounds at each door,
Leaving its card but it will come back
In remarkable guises, a wolf, a raven.
You will have to learn to live with it.

Like a cabin of hostages, reduced to adoring
A denimed bringer of horror or mercy, we wait,
Suspecting it's the god, the core
Out of which all, nothing is something is.

Déjeuner sur l'herbe

Mackenzie's shirtless,
Kneeling on rubbery
Grass to cadge some Thunderbird
Off Dougie, a novice
In translating the
Unenunciated word.

Mac's presided years
Over the crisp wrappers
Of a bachelors' picnic
On the flattened park verge,
Lacing his liquid
Takeaways with rhetoric;

This time passing out
Calm and cold, as the hunched
Accelerating homebound
Crowd ward off a hand-out
Of rain, eyes evading
The blessed body on the ground,

And the confrères, pissed-
On though they will be, wait
Until a man's comatose,
Breathing a bourn of mist,
Before they ransack
Wallet, carrier bag, clothes.

– Given what a round
Costs, merely practical:
Wheels within wheels, Dougie burrs,
Wills within wills it sounds
The way he says it,
As the three of them disperse.

Key

She walked up the High Road
In a dazzling June.
Lorries were backing to the timber yard,
Labourers left heel-crescents of mud, off home.

After the junction she stopped, and sensed –
Not "history", pack-camel to the mind's bazaar –
But that odder thing, from the first sea-cell,
To her, to the boy

Skating among push-chairs, to this:
Consciousness, growing words like skin.
She turned the key to the flat;
Let the High Road in.

Success

The bride fled for cover, in her cheap dress.
The groom kept walking, nearly eight feet tall,
And thin and mean from lack of tenderness.

I waited for my friends in the great hall,
When Peter Lorre came in with the groom.
Their plans betrayed no tenderness, at all.

I hid until a gendarme, fingering a knife,
Said you're not the one we're after, after all.
Down the seven landings I went running for my life,

Found an open door, a room of bric-à-brac:
Crisp antimacassars, needle-filled housewife,
Brass baby boots and Monarchs in shellac.

I'm safe, although embarrassed to impose.
The woman, Pat, pretends she doesn't mind.
She's a sometime star in Royal Variety Shows,

Does a few soaps, a little music hall.
I won't go out. I feel it, and she knows:
Outside there is no tenderness at all.

The Doctor as Oliver Reed

He washes his hands, tying rope knots
At a basin low as a urinal.
His back squares off territory.
His instruments: silver on velveteen,
The discretions of the anatomy room,
Fine-tuning his prognoses.
Restive under their ice-cream coats,
The students eye him like greyhounds.
Nurses turn silky; patients flush.
The man's sardonic with diseases,
It's said: scares them off,
Offering something kitsch and mouldy like cancer
A good stiff drink, or a duel.

Round

Out until 4 o'clock dancing, they're
Back on the ward at half-seven,
Vigorously turning the sheets.
I can't get up no

A double amputee fell
Off a wheelchair and began to spin
Until we could raise him.
I can't get up

A cancer case, deep yellow, spoke of
Discos at Barts, where he'd been a porter.
We slow slow danced, I braced him for x-ray.
no I can't get up

The sun floods the sluice room.
The young tree outside is a christening white.
He's drawn up his legs and stopped breathing.
no I can't get up

Neither Luke nor John
Nor Mary herself help the sister
To dial. Women shriek down the phone.
no

The Hetaira

We were becalmed in a safe harbour.
The passengers, important men in their suits,
Had been waiting for a whisper of wind.

Later we disembarked,
A boyish crew in our white vests and shorts, and led them
To the old town, through the ornamental gate.

I didn't know what I'd find when I looked for the haetera.
When we pulled back the curtain,
She was asleep on the floor of the cubicle,

Squat, distorted,
But agreeable to the price, as if she knew that her dancing
Would be necessary to us,

And that our procession,
Red from the light of the courtyard, could only pass here,
In the throat of her laughter.

Virginian Arcady

My muse came up from the creek,
Taller than a man in the speckled shade,
Where crayfish imitate tiny stones,
And the brisk water plays.

Reckon it was a muse, being so
Ringletty and fair, with a child's eye.
In her head-dress bitter, living grapes
Nest on the wild vine.

Strolling the bogged paths
Of the bottom field, apart by armslength,
She talked low, reproachful, pretty:
Said I don't love her enough.

Springfield, Virginia

Colonels live there, commuters to the Pentagon
In sweetly-named estates: King's Park, Orange Wood.
Springfield proper is a set of asphalt lots,
A catch-all town for realtors and mail.

At *Peoples Drug*, and the fast-food joints,
The hands popping open the cylinders of change
Hail from Vietnam or Nicaragua, arrivistes
Wondering at the sourness of God's people.

The high schoool kids who used to do the jobs
Were white, immune to history:
Andy Sulick, sheepish in a Big Ranch Stetson hat,
A row of enforced dim smiles at *Burger Chef*.

Eight hundred graduated in '71. That night,
Crawling the backroads, jumping in and out
Of unfamiliar cars, I found a party at a shack.
A boy mashed me against the lean-to floor.

Along the wooded road lightning bugs flared
Like drunks with matches, seeing their way home,
And whipperwills nagged the sleeper
Until a dawn as pink and blue as litmus paper.

Sunset Grill

EATS blinks red onto the parking lot.
The guy's guitar lets go
But Nadine don't wanna be true, whatever.
Rolling Rock's on special.

You OK?
She was right between them when it happened.
No time to duck or nothing.

His slim brown girlfriend slips off his knees.
It ain't easy dancing on peanut shells.
Play Hot Rod Lincoln.

I worked for him once and I can tell you straight...

She writes with a felt tip on a cocktail napkin,
Hair Fair   Brookfield Plaza
Ask for Renee.
Does it look that bad? he asks, gulping his beer.

The wired stand-up base
Cools, bum-bum, and the guitar
Loves us tonight
In Virginia, raining everywhere.

Country Pursuits

A horseshoe's a brute weight,
Nailed to a hoof between the farrier's knees,
Or flung with fine insouciance at a stake.
It can notch a scar, someone's boozy scoring.

At one wedding barbecue, combing the grass
Under the borrowed headlights of a truck,
As the last guest rocked and lurched along the drive,
The groom stepped back to stumble on his luck.

Seventeen Year Locust or Magicicada

As a nymph it latches for a stark
Seventeen years on a knuckled root,
Blind and hugely feeding
Hostage to the dark.

A swelling ache
Corkscrews it from the ground,
To hug the nearest vertical,
Squaddie out of bivouac,

And burst the carcass, dangled
Like a pilot from a one-seater
With flaccid wings, bug eyes,
And goggled head.

Hardening, it starts to pull
Free; by dawn it flies,
Fuelled just long enough for sex:
A single churring in the red maple.

Corn Palace

The façade of the Corn Palace, in Mitchell, South Dakota,
Depicts, with grains and grasses – maize, and wheat –
Sodbusters in a Connestoga wagon.
Postcards may be bought, next to the beer.

White-toothed Scandinavian blondes
Test the compass-points of the flat grid
In heavy family cars, driving on
And hailing teenage friends,

While chains of light go up along the Corn Palace
Celebrating the achievement of noise
At Mitchell, like a bubbling spa, set
In fields that are dark for miles and miles.

Camano, Puget Sound

Swollen with rain and ash,
The cliff weighs on its bulkheads.
They tilt across a littering of shells
Like heavy guns. Out on the Sound

The silhouette of a small boat
Merges with its slight verticals:
Your sons, my husband casting out.
We're left on shore to watch

The dips and surfacings of seals,
A dogfish, silvering its back,
And the light breaks wide, until it hurts,
Until we shade our eyes.

Mount Rainier

On seven broad lanes,
In a borrowed Cabriolet,
Choosing between solar windows
And thunderous moving air,
I saw it beside us, westerly,
Displacing sky.

It had been rumoured
During the visit, a week of mists.
We carried the image south
To the dry light of the mesa;
Down the courseways
Of green, tropic swamps.

Wrapped in a killing wind,
It shines on the small sights
And the flatlands –
While in the furious cars,
They are learning
That they'll come back.

Bay of Pigs

This house of ours is peacock blue
At sundown with the trees and air.
The street boils dry by every noon.
I went to the ocean to look at the sand.
The footmarks were colossal,
The man as tall as a flagpole.
Do you want we can teach you the rumba –
Laughing with his great teeth closed.
I think he was American.
The morning sky went black as bruise.
I ran away from there so scared
And sirens crossed the air and clouds
In doomsday squads. It was nightmare.

Daytrip

We'd left the cameras in the Hertz
But made St. P's for the tourist Passion.
I knew one of the trio:
This is what he did on his vacations.
The bearded heads bled from the corbels.
We walked by the pleated steps of a temple
In whose maw the usual type was being tried with flame.

We took in the long galleria before lunch.
Sloan made some remark about art being *vox populi*.
I sent him back to the Excelsior with a flea in his ear.
The roofs stretched out, pale in the heat and peaceable.
Your shoulder touched mine. I could tell you were moved.
The wine and the drowse of pigeons dismissed
Any rancour between us. Rested we'd be as good as gold.

Homage to Jean Rhys

At the corner table, perusing a face
In unimproving colours,
Brandy, absinthe, Cinzano,

Latticed by the rudeness
Of strangers, shut portcullis,
Madam whispers

To a passing gentleman
Who has, he's afraid, to dash:
Words are bandages.

The reader peers, permitted like
A medical student.
She's forgotten him.

Swaddled tight, she'll black out
Harmlessly, unhelped:
A walking Montmartre ghost,

Ex-chorus girl, anglaise,
Vieille, ex-ex.
No one can get in or out.

A Sight in Macao

She crosses to them, dragging the foot
A swan trails in water.
On the steps up to the Catholic fathers,
The young mark a new year
In sparklers fizzing out lithe
Dragons of smoke. Her views of the dud façade
Were snapped after dawn; blue; unpeopled.

They're businessman, the smiling guarded pair.
They'd choose to see her
As the available East, or even simpler –
Observing the lameness – as asking for money.
But now her views are theirs,
Tinting memory, to be mailed to Dubuque or Boston,
And she resumes her watchfulness.

The Uni-Gym

At a shout to a disco drum, the women dance
In sorbet cotton knits. Sweat darkening
On spines, they bend and reach.

In the stone chill of the gym downstairs,
Weightlifters howl, as if for sex,
Or pace, furtive in the room-sized mirror,

To meet gingerly in bed. His density
Helps him feel safer from the likes of her –
Whose heart is stronger now, and unforgiving.

Flynn

I saw Flynn from the 14 bus
Launched from Mecca's,
Trudging towards Kings Cross.

He's been livelier, last week
Gesturing hugely in the bra boutique
(I kissed him, had to take it back.)

I mouthe while his body talks, shameless.
Tight shoulders, sentry's head –
We've gone further than he intended.

Even crying in my arms, any sense of us
Eludes him like luxury. I rap the glass
With my ring. He doesn't see me.

Destiny, Limited

Here is high street frontage,
A dark suggestive curtain behind glass
And a neat white card announcing
Dignity in Destiny, Limited. A place of rest.
It is hard to imagine feeling that tired.

Even our man McBrain, jesuitical atheist,
Can't unpick the stitch more private than sex
Or unwish the angels that jig on the needle
At bedside or trench, saying comfortable words,
Lurid and used as dirty magazines.

Each hope has its use – dignity wished
On the arrested corpse; on the newborn,
Time wrapped pulsing around its neck;
On moments that burst and rise as breath,
Emptied, to the needle's eye.

Sister Dread

The future unself, that starts with me,
The sexless yellowing sister,
Bored with her safe plot under the roses,
Sets me problems of the cryptic type.
She fancies herself a teacher.

How gratifying to see me sweat.
She's a bundle of sticks, no monster.
Having to go through the stage of effluvium
She hates the smell:
I stick in the craw of her tidy eternity.

She thinks she is omnivorous, although
I have my unassailable territory.
Reduced to pulling hideous faces through glass,
She'd prefer to believe that I never was
Her sitting tenant, but fact is fact.

Athletic

I've stripped down to the clean athletic.
Even blood relatives fall away. Their trace
Is a spidery map of obligations,
And a compass needle, flitting towards normalcy.
I have my deadlines; my coldwater diet.
The early freshness has burned off,
Although the heart works double time.
Power is its priority, not love.
It is red and rude to the egg's melancholy,
Sacrificing her gladly. My face fits me,
These days, like a glove of pig leather,
And hides the arrogant boy
With the fear of long meetings.
The one thing he knows how to do is destroy.

Faith Healers

This could be the mind's antechamber:
Skylight, pre-war folding chairs, a stand of books,
The *Psychic News*, a hand-penned plea, DONATIONS:
Against each wall a lame hope waiting.

The ends of her sparse hair are a failed red,
She's stout and leads a shambling Alsatian.
'Through the veil' a limpid Jesus lifts his eyes
Above the nursery warmth, the funk of flowers.

The heaters of the clerestory
Burn among the eaves, vivid as lollies.
Patients play stone crusaders on the spindly beds.
The healers in their grocery macs

Press forehead, gut and thighs
Like John who spent his grace on strays
In a sirocco, a name for talisman.
They tend the dog, lay hands on anyone.

A Stroll

Her hips strain through the dress,
Carmen red to his sober stylishness,
Camden caballero in a black hat.
Nothing can bother them. They chat
Like starlings, heading for the White
Hart past every peril: blind traffic light,
An alcoholic bear, newsagents with two heads,
The neutral shopfront of the dead,
Shyly touting its enforced occasions
Of funerals, embalming and cremations.

Streambed

What was once bird
Is a fan of grey feathers,
Wavering on the streambed,
A few feet from the Thames.

It ate a barleycorn, and now
The green blade is eating it,
Vivid and cruel
As some young can be.

The blue-lit chub
Course through the shallows.
The down flutters,
Pinioned by the shoots.

An old party on the footbridge
Lingering after others,
Following the fish,
Ignores the former bird.

Fortuna

Of the countries, no one had their pick:
They lugged their bundles to the dock,
And sailed at night as if by magic.

Inland, a label flickered on a tree
In every plot. They heaped up turf
With an obstinate energy,

Plied against the sudden gun,
Or the slow match between warders
For what they'd never done.

Memo to Auden

Wystan, you got off to a wrong start
Being neither Catholic nor tubercular,
Nor a brash, alert provincial,
But you righted like a figure-skater
And traced your syntactical curlicues
Tight and fine, too make them news.

Out of the wry side of your mouth,
You dropped a flagrant quote or two.
With my dog-eared copy for credential,
I'd like to pick a minor bone with you.
Just pretend I'm fresh at public school
And try to keep your prefectorial cool.

Do you recall the Christ Church coffee shop?
You'd agreed to sit there daily
At four o'clock and dawdle, bored,
A big cat, for an exhibition fee:
Available for metric consultation
To any undergrad with nerve, or vision.

Gaping there, I lost an opportunity.
In fact I spilled Darjeeling on your shoe
(Smart Oxford brogue) and nearly missed
Watching the Jo'burg tourist corner you.
He brought a semaphoric forearm down
To shake your hand, quite heedless of your frown,

Luminous with praise,
And bombast and italicised exclaiming.
Your work had meant a lot to him, especially
That famous poem I'd re-offend by naming –
No gavel-wielding judge has ever rapped it
So sharply as Your Honour did: 'I scrapped it.'

Now to the old gnawed bone, that poetry
Makes nothing happen, the report
Of someone flatly sidelined by a war,
Who feels embarrassed holding down the fort –
Unheroically and not from duty –
Of common intellect and beauty.

The worst horrors can't be quantified,
Can't be healed, denied, forgot,
But implicit in the name of peace
Are its varied fruits, that rot
Under a swastika; its vines that die
Tied to the paling of a lie.

What is the alternative to art?
Religion of guns, guns of religion.
You know all this. You said it well,
But you have a grumpy disposition,
So I'm repeating, like an awkward kid,
What you tell us, Dad, ain't what you did.

In the careful mornings of the art
Over tonic cuppas in the lav,
Not to speak of sweaty collaboration
With Isherwood, Kallman, Britten, Strav,
You didn't do it for the bread alone:
Poets have to charm their bread from stone.

You didn't do it for the pick-up trade:
Most were arty foreigners, not rough.
You liked a wholesome share of fame
But found the poet tag absurd enough
When talking with commercial sorts on trains.
Other professions call for verve and brains,

But you chose this one. Why?
Words are saucy, difficult but willing.
You could play boss and close the study door.
But there was another end, as thrilling
When the scholar's breath went sour:
Coaxing lines from beauty gave her power,

And this was the Holy: an act of love
To damn the bunker, damn the bomb
And celebrate the individual life
Of myriad relations, from a room
Where the isolate voice is listened to
Through all its range, by such as you.

Let the victims, and their helpers,
And the guilty rest there for a time.
Let there be a commonality of good,
Gardens, architecture, rhyme,
That we betray by happenstance,
Forgiving airs to make us dance.

P.S. Myself I have too much to learn
Of voice and sense. You used this metre,
Don Juan too, but in our day
It's not exactly a world-beater.
Still, "subtle" can mean convoluted
And for our little chat, it suited.